SUPER SPORTS STAR
KEVIN GARNETT

Stew Thornley

Enslow Publishers, Inc.

40 Industrial Road   PO Box 38
Box 398   Aldershot
Berkeley Heights, NJ 07922   Hants GU12 6BP
USA   UK

http://www.enslow.com

Library of Congress Cataloging-in-Publication Data

Thornley, Stew.
    Super sports star Kevin Garnett / Stew Thornley.
        p. cm. — (Super sports star)
Includes bibliographical references and index.
Summary: Profiles the power forward for the Minnesota Timberwolves, discussing his childhood in South Carolina and high school years in Chicago, his decision to skip college, and his success with the Timberwolves.
    ISBN 0-7660-1515-7
    1. Garnett, Kevin, 1976—Juvenile literature. 2. Basketball players—United States—Biography—Juvenile literature. [1. Garnett, Kevin, 1976– . 2. Basketball players. 3. Afro-Americans—Biography.]
I. Title. II. Series.
    GV884.G37   T56   2001
    796.323'092—dc21
    [B]   00-009120

Printed in the United States of America

10 9 8 7 6 5 4 3 2 1

To Our Readers:
All Internet Addresses in this book were active and appropriate when we went to press. Any comments or suggestions can be sent by e-mail to Comments@enslow.com or to the address on the back cover.

CONTENTS

Introduction 4

1 Leading the Way 7

2 Spending Time on the Court 10

3 Playing to Win 15

4 A Hot Rookie 25

5 Making It in Minnesota 31

6 Moving On Up 37

Career Statistics 42

Where to Write 43

Words to Know 44

Reading About and
Internet Addresses 46

Index 48

Introduction

Fans get excited when Kevin Garnett plays. They cheer, scream, clap, and stomp their feet. They may also shout Garnett's name. Sometimes they scream just his initials—K. G.

Garnett also gets excited during games. He may even shout out his own name when he is angry with himself. "C'mon, K. G.," he hollers when he misses a shot.

When Garnett dunks, he yells on his way down from the basket. It keeps him excited. This excitement rubs off on his teammates. As one of his teammates said, "Kevin's enthusiasm toward the game is something special."

Garnett plays for the

Sometimes Kevin Garnett shouts out his own name during a game. When he misses a shot he might yell "C'mon, K.G."

Minnesota Timberwolves. He is known as "Da Kid," which means "the kid." Garnett joined the National Basketball Association (NBA) when he was only nineteen years old. He was six feet ten inches tall and still growing.

Even though Kevin Garnett is big, he plays a position called small forward. A small forward has to be able to score points for his team. He has to be able to shoot from the outside, a long distance from the basket. He also has to be able to pass the ball well. Kevin Garnett can do all of these things.

Kevin Garnett can also do the things a center or power forward has to do. He can block shots and grab rebounds. He can play defense, and he can dunk the ball through the hoop.

Garnett is quick and he can dribble the ball, too. There is no question about it: Kevin Garnett is one of the best players in the NBA.

Leading the Way

CHAPTER
1

The Minnesota Timberwolves were trying to earn a playoff spot. They were playing against the Golden State Warriors. It was one of the last games of the 1999 season and the Timberwolves needed to win. But late in the game, Golden State had the lead. The score was 72–70, and Minnesota had the ball. Then Kevin Garnett called to a teammate to pass the ball to him. When Garnett caught the pass, he had his back to the basket. He dribbled and backed up. A defender tried to stop him, but Garnett got closer to the basket. He turned and jumped. The defender also jumped and tried to stop Garnett. The defender's move did not work. Garnett reached up and dunked the ball. The game was tied.

Minnesota got the ball back and charged

down the court. Garnett got the ball again. This time, he jumped up to take the shot, and the ball dropped through the basket. Minnesota took the lead.

Garnett kept scoring in the final minutes. He also played well on defense. Donyell Marshall of the Warriors missed a long shot. It was Kevin Garnett who reached out with his long arms and grabbed the ball. That was just one of 15 rebounds he had in the game.

Later, Garnett was fouled. He went to the free-throw line and sank two shots. That put Minnesota ahead, 86–81. There were only twelve seconds left in the game and Minnesota went on to win.

Kevin Garnett scored 28 points in the game. He had 12 points in the final four minutes. He played his best when his team needed him the most. That is the sign of a leader.

CHAPTER 2

Spending Time on the Court

Kevin Garnett was born on May 19, 1976. He grew up in Mauldin, South Carolina, a small town near Greenville.

Kevin's dad, O'Lewis McCullough, had been a good basketball player. McCullough had been known as "Bye-Bye 45." His number in high school was 45, and he was very fast. He would steal the ball and take off running down the court toward the basket. When that happened, it was "Bye-Bye 45."

Kevin's father did not live with him, though. Ernest Irby was Kevin's stepfather. Irby did not like basketball. He would not let Kevin have a basketball hoop in the driveway. That did not keep Kevin from playing basketball, though. He loved the game.

Baron Franks was one of Kevin Garnett's friends. Franks said about Garnett, "All he did was talk about basketball. And every time you saw him, he had a ball. Sun up. Sun down. Up and down the street. All day long."

Franks was known as "Bear." He was several

years older than Garnett. He was also bigger. Kevin and Bear would often play basketball against each other. Bear would not go easy on Kevin. He wore Kevin out on the court. Garnett sometimes wondered if Franks liked him. Bear Franks did like Kevin Garnett, but he wanted to help him improve his game. The tough treatment on the court was his way of teaching Kevin. And Kevin did get better. He also got tougher. Playing against Bear helped him a lot.

Kevin also played basketball

Kevin Garnett towers over his defenders on the court.

with other friends at Springfield Park in Mauldin. Kevin's best friend was Jaime Peters. Peters was known as "Bug." Kevin and Bug were about the same age. Their houses were across the street from one another in Mauldin.

Bug was small and not very good at basketball, but he knew that Kevin had talent. He encouraged Kevin to play basketball. The two went to Springfield Park together all the time.

Kevin spent a lot of time at the park. Even after everyone else left, Kevin stayed. He would shoot baskets by himself under the lights.

Kevin also had other things to do besides play basketball. He took care of his younger sister, Ashley. Kevin also had an older sister, Sonya. Their mother, Shirley, worked two jobs to support them. She worked in a factory and also had a hair-styling business. She was away from home a lot, so Kevin helped out with his younger sister.

Kevin still found lots of time to play

basketball, though. He could not get enough of it. When he was in ninth grade, his first year of high school, he tried out for the high school team. His mother did not even know he had tried out. By the time she found out, Kevin had already made the team.

Playing to Win

Kevin Garnett was tall when he started high school. In ninth grade, he was six feet seven inches tall. He was already a good defensive player. With his long arms he could easily block shots. He could also jump and grab rebounds, too.

He needed to work on his offense, though. He tried hard to improve, and it paid off. His coach at Mauldin High School was James "Duke" Fisher. Coach Fisher taught Garnett how to dribble, pass, and shoot. The coach was impressed with how hard Garnett worked to improve. Garnett had a good year during his first year of high school. He scored an average of 12.5 points per game. He also averaged 14 rebounds and 7 blocked shots. Those were good totals, but Kevin Garnett was only getting started.

Coach Fisher said Garnett was a team player. "He didn't care who scored," said Fisher. "That is the truth. The only thing he hated was

In high school, Kevin Garnett played basketball all year—even in the summer. All that practice has definitely paid off for the Minnesota Timberwolves.

to lose." With Kevin Garnett playing, the Mauldin Mavericks did not lose much.

Fans in Mauldin were excited about the team. By Kevin Garnett's third year in high school, it was hard to get a ticket to see the team play. The gym at Mauldin High School was full for every game. Many fans could not get into the gym. They crowded into the hallway outside the gym. They could not see the game, but they could hear it. That was good enough for them.

In his third year in high school, Garnett averaged 27 points, 17 rebounds, and 7 blocks. He was named Mr. Basketball for South Carolina. Mr. Basketball is the award given to the best high school player in the state.

Garnett played basketball all year. He even played in a summer league. His coach in that league was Darren "Bull" Gazaway. Gazaway had been coaching summer basketball for many years. He put together a great team in 1994, the summer after Kevin's third year in high school.

The team went to the Kentucky Hoopfest Tournament held in Louisville. Other great teams from many states came too. But the team that Kevin played on was the best. Kevin's team won the Hoopfest championship.

Kevin Garnett also played in many other competitions around the United States. The teams were put together with the best high school players in the country. Garnett did

Kevin Garnett shows off his style on the court.

well in these tournaments. He attracted a lot of attention.

But Kevin Garnett was a private person. He did not like all the attention. He wanted to blend in. He found a way to do that when he changed to a high school in a much larger city. Garnett, his mother, and younger sister moved to Chicago. He attended Farragut Academy.

Farragut's coach was William "Wolf" Nelson. Kevin Garnett had met him in the summer of 1994, at a basketball camp in Chicago. Garnett decided he would like to play for Coach Nelson.

Kevin Garnett and his family even lived in the same apartment building where Coach Nelson lived. It was not in a nice part of town, though. There were street gangs in the area. It was not safe to go out alone at night. Garnett learned it was different from Mauldin, South Carolina, where he could go to the park at night. In Chicago, he had to stay home.

Chicago is the home of the Bears football

team. The Bears are known as "Da Bears." It is also home to the Chicago Bulls basketball team. The Bulls are known as "Da Bulls." When Kevin Garnett got to Chicago, he became known as "Da Kid." It is a name he still has today.

One of Kevin Garnett's teammates at Farragut was Ronnie Fields. Garnett had met Fields at basketball camp in Chicago. Ronnie Fields was a great jumper. He also had some interesting moves.

With Kevin Garnett and Ronnie Fields, the Farragut Admirals team was one of the best in the state. It was even one of the top teams in the country.

Kevin Garnett was again the leader of his team. He was still playing in front of large crowds. In January 1995, Farragut played against a good team from the town of Rock Island, near Chicago. More than five thousand fans were at the Farragut gym for the game. Ronnie Fields and Kevin Garnett put on a great show. Fields had some amazing dunks. But

Kevin Garnett earned the nickname "Da Kid," when he played high school basketball for Farragut Academy in Chicago. "Da Kid" shows off his moves as he goes up for the score.

Garnett also thrilled the fans with a few slam dunks. He scored 23 points and had 19 rebounds in the game. Farragut beat Rock Island by twelve points.

Kevin Garnett again played well a few weeks later. The Admirals were playing Carver High School of Chicago in a championship game. Garnett had 32 points and 13 rebounds. Farragut won, 71–62.

The Farragut Admirals went to the state tournament. The team did not win, but Kevin Garnett played well. When the season was over, Garnett was named Mr. Basketball for Illinois. He had now won that award in South Carolina and Illinois.

Everyone knew Kevin Garnett

Kevin Garnett is airborne, on his way to another crowd-pleasing dunk shot.

was a great star. Now he had to make a choice. Would he go to college or begin to play professional basketball?

Teams from the NBA had been watching him. A lot of teams wanted Kevin Garnett to play for them. He decided he would go play basketball in the NBA. "I went with my heart," he said.

Many people did not think Kevin Garnett was ready to play with the pros. Some people thought Garnett was making a mistake by not going to college first. But Garnett knew he could prove them wrong.

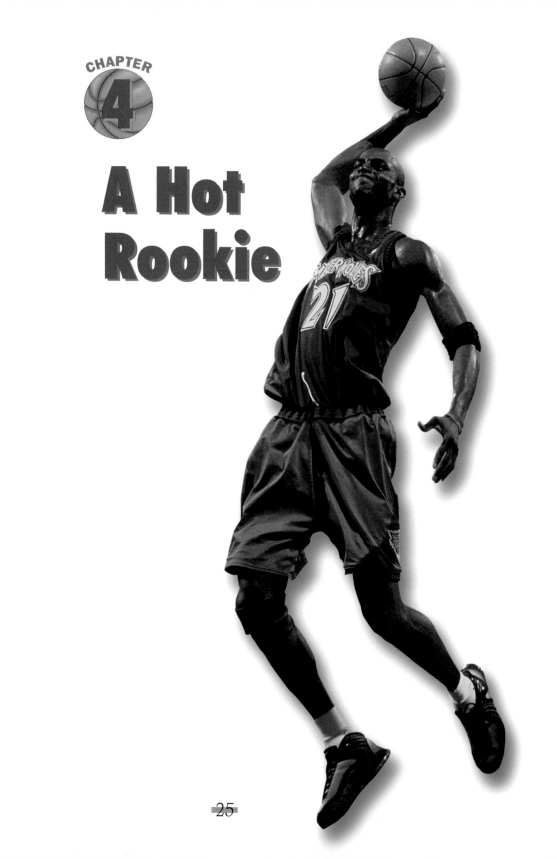

A Hot Rookie

The NBA draft is the way that professional basketball teams choose new players each year. Teams take turns picking players. There were a lot of good players waiting to be chosen in June 1995. Damon Stoudamire, Joe Smith, Antonio McDyess, and Jerry Stackhouse were among them. They had all played basketball in college. Kevin Garnett was different. He was coming to the NBA right after high school.

Even so, Garnett was the fifth player chosen. The Minnesota Timberwolves picked him. They thought he would become a great player, maybe even a superstar. But they knew that would not happen right away.

The Timberwolves wanted Garnett to get used to playing in the NBA. He would be playing against better players than the ones he had seen in high school. He would also be traveling a lot. And he would be living in Minnesota, far away from his family. All this would be new to Kevin Garnett.

Garnett spent a lot of time sitting on the

Kevin Garnett showed a lot of people that he could play in the NBA. He also showed the Timberwolves he could be a big help to the team.

sideline, not playing. But when he got the chance, he showed how good he could be. A few weeks into the 1995 season, Minnesota played the Vancouver Grizzlies. Early in the second quarter, a Vancouver player missed a shot. Kevin Garnett grabbed the rebound. He turned and threw a pass out of the crowd of players. Then he raced down the court. His long legs carried him past defenders. Garnett crossed midcourt. He looked for the ball. A teammate threw a pass to him. Garnett caught it, got set, and took a shot. The long shot dropped through the basket. It was such a long shot that it was worth three points.

Garnett's play excited the other players on the Timberwolves. Minnesota went on to win the game by more than twenty points.

Garnett was showing a lot of people that he could play in the NBA. A game between Houston and Minnesota in March 1996 proved Garnett was ready for the NBA. The score was close in the fourth quarter, then Garnett got

Moves like these helped Kevin Garnett earn a spot in the starting lineup during the 1995–96 season.

going. He scored nine straight points in two minutes. In that time, he also had 2 rebounds and blocked 2 shots.

During the 1995–96 season, the Timberwolves traded Christian Laettner to the Atlanta Hawks. The trade opened up a spot in the starting lineup. Timberwolves' coach Flip Saunders thought Kevin Garnett was the man to fill that spot. So, Garnett got more playing time. Three weeks later, Garnett scored 33 points in a game against the Boston Celtics.

Kevin Garnett started in all of Minnesota's games over the last half of the season. During that time, he averaged 14 points per game.

"The first time I saw him work out, I thought he had a chance to be great," said Coach Saunders. But Kevin Garnett was becoming a great player even faster than Saunders thought he would.

Making It in Minnesota

Kevin Garnett had a new teammate during his second season in the NBA. It was someone he already knew. Stephon Marbury and Kevin Garnett had met two years earlier, and they quickly became friends. They often talked on the phone. They once played on the same team in the High School All-Star Game in Chicago. In that game, Marbury threw a pass toward the basket. Garnett jumped, grabbed the ball, and slammed it in the basket for the score. That was an event that would be repeated in the NBA.

The Timberwolves drafted Stephon Marbury as their first pick in the 1996 NBA draft. Marbury was a point guard. It was his job to pass the ball. Kevin Garnett was the perfect target for Marbury's passes.

Garnett and Marbury were a great pair. They thrilled the fans in Minnesota's arena, the Target Center. It was also a good year for Garnett and the rest of the team. Garnett played in 77 games. He started in all of them.

With the help of strong play by Kevin Garnett, Minnesota made the playoffs during the 1996–97 season.

He also played in the NBA All-Star Game where he had 6 points and 9 rebounds.

With Stephon Marbury and Kevin Garnett, the Timberwolves had their best season ever. Minnesota made the playoffs for the first time in its history. The Timberwolves played the Houston Rockets. The Rockets had many great players. Hakeem Olajuwon, Clyde Drexler, and Charles Barkley were all on the Rockets at that time. The Timberwolves counted on young players like Kevin Garnett and Stephon Marbury. Houston won the playoff series, but Kevin Garnett played well.

During the next season, Garnett had another big game against Houston. It came in February 1998. Minnesota had just gotten bad news. Their power forward, Tom Gugliotta, had hurt his ankle. The Timberwolves found out he would miss the rest of the season.

Garnett would have to play well, and he did. Against the Rockets, Garnett did it all. He scored 25 points and had 17 rebounds. He had 4

Kevin Garnett fights for position under the basket.

assists and he blocked 2 shots. Garnett guarded smaller players like Clyde Drexler. He used his long arms to make Drexler miss shots. Garnett also guarded bigger players like Charles Barkley and Hakeem Olajuwon. He used his strength to take rebounds away from them. Minnesota beat the Rockets in overtime. Overtime is extra time added on to the end of a game that ends with a tie score.

Kevin Garnett started in all of Minnesota's games during the 1997–98 season. He scored in double figures in every game. That means he had 10 or more points in every game. Garnett also played in the NBA All-Star Game again. He scored 12 points.

Kevin Garnett was still young. But already he was a big man on the court.

Moving On Up

Kevin Garnett played better than ever in the 1999 season. He needed to play well because Minnesota had traded away Stephon Marbury to the New Jersey Nets.

Garnett led his team in scoring with an average of 20.8 points per game. He also averaged 10.4 rebounds per game.

That was the best rebounding average on the Timberwolves, and ninth-best in the entire league. In April 1999, Garnett was named NBA Player of the Week. He led the Timberwolves to three wins in one week.

Minnesota made the playoffs for the third year in a row. They played the San Antonio Spurs. San Antonio had two great players, David Robinson and Tim Duncan. Robinson and Duncan are both over seven feet tall.

The Spurs won the first game in the playoffs. In the second game, though, the Timberwolves won. Kevin Garnett played against Tim Duncan and he did well. He also guarded some of the other Spurs players.

★★★★ UP CLOSE

In the summer when the basketball season is over, Kevin Garnett goes back to South Carolina. He has a house there, too. He often plays basketball with high school kids in Mauldin. After the game, he takes them out to eat. Garnett's favorite foods are hamburgers, french fries, and pizza. He also likes chicken and fish.

In the fourth quarter, Minnesota had a four-point lead. Then Kevin Garnett hit three baskets in a row. The lead for Minnesota was then 10 points. San Antonio tried to come back. Tim Duncan threw a pass down the court. But Kevin Garnett reached out and tapped it away. Minnesota won the game.

San Antonio went on to win the playoff series and the NBA championship. But Kevin Garnett and the Timberwolves had played well.

In 2000, Kevin Garnett and the rest of the Timberwolves played well enough to reach the first round of the playoffs. But Minnesota lost to the Portland Trail Blazers in four games.

UP CLOSE

Kevin Garnett never went to college, but he has promised his mother that he will continue his education someday. He started studying business by mail with the University of Minnesota.

When he is not playing basketball, Garnett stays close to home. He may spend time with close friends. He has a big house in Minnesota. Some of his friends from South Carolina live with him. These are the people he trusts. He knows they like him because he is a nice person. They are not friends with him just because he is famous.

Kevin Garnett is serious about basketball. He works hard to be the best player he can be. But he also knows how to have a good time. "I'm still a kid," Garnett says. "I'm having fun all the time."

CAREER STATISTICS

	NBA								
Team	Year	GP	FG%	FT%	REB	AST	STL	BLK	PPG
Timberwolves	1995–96	80	.491	.705	501	145	86	131	10.4
Timberwolves	1996–97	77	.499	.754	618	236	105	163	17.0
Timberwolves	1997–98	82	.491	.738	786	348	139	150	18.5
Timberwolves	1998–99	47	.460	.704	489	202	78	83	20.8
Timberwolves	1999–2000	81	.497	.765	956	401	120	126	22.9
Totals		367	.489	.740	3,350	1,332	528	653	17.7

GP—Games Played
FG%—Field Goal Percentage
FT%—Free Throw Percentage
REB—Rebounds
AST—Assists
STL—Steals
BLK—Blocked Shots
PPG—Points Per Game

Where to Write to Kevin Garnett

Mr. Kevin Garnett
Minnesota Timberwolves
Target Center
600 First Ave. North
Minneapolis, MN 55403-9801

WORDS TO KNOW

assist—A pass to a teammate who makes a basket.

baseline—The out-of-bounds line that runs behind the basket.

double-teaming—Two defenders guarding one player.

draft—The way NBA teams choose new players each year.

dunk—A shot that is slammed through the basket from directly above the basket. It is also known as a slam or slam dunk.

fadeaway—A shot taken while falling away from the basket.

jump hook—A one-handed shot taken while jumping.

outside shot—A shot taken a long distance away from the basket.

rebound—Grabbing the basketball after a missed shot.

turnaround—A shot taken after the player has turned to face the basket.

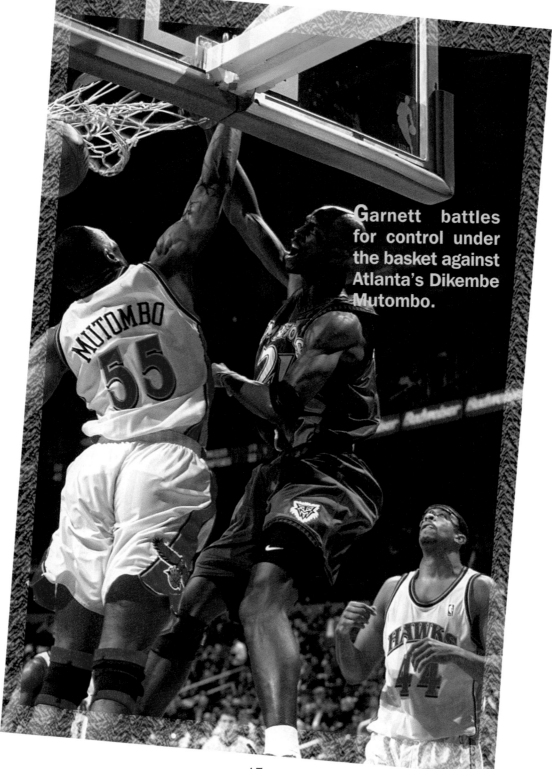

Garnett battles for control under the basket against Atlanta's Dikembe Mutombo.

READING ABOUT

Books

"Who Are the Best Rookies?, *Sports Illustrated for Kids*, December 1995, p. 36

Dougherty, Terri. *Kevin Garnett*. Minneapolis, Minn.: ABDO Publishing Co., Inc., 1999.

Macnow, Glenn. *Sports Great Kevin Garnett*. Springfield, N.J.: Enslow Publishers, Inc., 2000.

Torres, John A. *Kevin Garnett: "Da Kid."* Minneapolis, Minn.: Lerner Publications, 1999.

Internet Addresses

The Official Site of the NBA
<http://www.nba.com/playerfile/kevin_garnett.html>

The Official Site of the Minnesota Timberwolves
<http://www.nba.com/timberwolves/>

Kevin Garnett works wonders on the court.

INDEX

B

Barkley, Charles, 34, 36
Boston Celtics, 30

C

Chicago Bears, 21
Chicago Bulls, 21

D

Drexler, Clyde, 34, 36
Duncan, Tim, 39

F

Fields, Ronnie, 21
Fisher, James "Duke," 16
Franks, Baron "Bear," 11–12

G

Garnett, Shirley (mother), 13
Gazaway, Darren "Bull," 18
Golden State Warriors, 8
Gugliotta, Tom, 34

H

Harris, Sonya (sister), 13
Houston Rockets, 34

I

Irby, Ernest (stepfather), 11

K

Kentucky Hoopfest
    Tournament, 19

L

Laettner, Christian, 30

M

Marbury, Stephon, 32, 34, 38
Marshall, Donyell, 9
McCullough, O'Lewis
    (father), 11
McDyess, Antonio, 26
Minnesota Timberwolves, 6, 26

N

National Basketball Association
    (NBA), 6
Nelson, William "Wolf," 20
New Jersey Nets, 38

O

Olajuwon, Hakeem, 34, 36

P

Peters, Jaime "Bug," 13
Phelps, Ashley (sister), 13
Portland Trail Blazers, 40

R

Robinson, David, 39

S

San Antonio Spurs, 39
Saunders, Phil "Flip," 30
Smith, Joe, 26
Stackhouse, Jerry, 26
Stoudamire, Damon, 26

V

Vancouver Grizzlies, 28